What To Do in Tough Times

by
Tom Leding

TLM Publishing
Tulsa, Oklahoma

The majority of scriptures in this book are from *The King James Version of the Holy Bible* (KJV). Other scriptures are from *The New American Standard Bible* (NAS), (La Habra, CA: The Lockman Foundation, 1960-1977); and *The New International Version* (NIV), (Grand Rapids: Zondervan Publishing House, 1973, 1978, 1984).

What To Do in Tough Times
ISBN 1-890915-13-0
Copyright © 2005 by Tom Leding
TLM Publishing
4412 S. Harvard
Tulsa, OK 74135
Printed in the United States of America

Contents

Tough Times Are Not New

Well-known radio commentator and author Paul Harvey once said, "In times like these, it helps to recall that there have always been times like these."[1]

The late noted film star Mary Pickford wrote during the Great Depression years in her book, *Why Not Try God?*:

> Today is a new day. You will get out of it just what you put into it. If you have made mistakes, even serious mistakes, there is always another chance for you. And supposing you have tried and failed again and again, you may have a fresh start any moment you choose, for this thing that we call "failure" is not the falling down, but the staying down.[2]

[1] John Maxwell, *Leadership 101*, (Tulsa: Honor Books, Copyright 1994 by John C. Maxwell), p. 88.
[2] Pickford, Mary, *Why Not Try God?*, 1934, quoted in *100 Voices*, (Bloomington, MN: Copyright 1999 by FrontPorch Books, a division of Garborg's, Inc.), p. 48.

The late great evangelist Dwight L. Moody once said, "Character is what a man is in the dark." It is just as true to say, "Character is what a man or woman is in tough times."[3]

---

[3]Van Crouch. *Winning 101* (Tulsa: Honor Books, Copyright by William V. Crouch, 1995), p. 66.

Don't Forget:
This Too Will Pass

It may seem odd to talk about tough times when many have prophesied we are in a "time of overflow," that these are good times. However, that will not be true for everyone, not even every Christian, only for those who have sowed finances, time, prayer, and obedience in previous years.

There will be tough times for some, even in a "time of overflow." On the other hand, there always is what amounts to good situations for some in the middle of tough times.

The definition of "overflow" changes when tough times involve an entire community or nation such as the 1930-1939 years of the Great Depression. Tough times then meant a national environment of poverty, panic, fear, and deprivation.

Overflow meant having enough to eat, being able to keep your home, walking in the peace of God, and having enough for yourself, your family, and to help others. That was true prosperity in tough times. There were people who lived like that.

Yet there also were thousands of suicides as people gave in to despair. Businesses failed, banks closed, and unemployment went to 25 percent. On the other hand, 75 percent of people kept their jobs, child labor was outlawed, and modern inventions were developed such as the jet engine. Life went on even if not as usual.

Modern American Christians tend to define "overflow" as material prosperity, having more money, more goods, and more success. Christians in Third World countries might define "overflow" as a bicycle, a house, and more than enough food.

No human being ever goes through life always experiencing good times. That old saying, "Into each life some rain must fall," really means "Into each life some rain *will* fall." Or, we could say, "God never promised us a rose garden."

In fact, you might say we are promised or warned about the exact opposite state of affairs. (James 1:2-4; Heb. 12:7.)

However, God has given the greatest assurance that we will come through victorious *if* we focus on Him: **Many are the afflictions of the righteous, but the Lord delivereth him out of them all . . . The Lord redeemeth the soul of his servants; and none of them who trust in him shall be desolate** (Ps. 34:19,22.)

Why do the righteous have "many afflictions"? Tough times come because the disobedience of our first ancestors has had consequences. The first consequence was the forfeiture of their dominion or stewardship of earth to Satan. (Gen. 3:16-24.)

Since the times of the garden east of Eden (Gen.1-3), man has lived in a world largely operating under systems of government, education, economics, culture and entertainment ruled by anti-godly principles.

Sooner or later, they will fail. How soon depends on how much they adhere to the ways and principles of the one Jesus called the "Prince of This World Order." (John 12:31, 14:30, 16:11.)

Yes, Satan was defeated by Jesus on the cross (Col. 2:14,15) and was "cast out" (John

12:31), but not yet permanently to "the bottomless pit." (Rev. 20:1-3,10.) However, the systems influenced by him (called "the world, the flesh, and the devil") have continued and will continue until Jesus returns.

Our world systems range from partly good to partly bad to all bad. None are all good, in the sense of totally operating on God's principles. Therefore, sooner or later, they will fail, resulting in a lesser or greater amount of tough times.

There is no "happily ever after" until Jesus returns and all things are put under His feet in reality. (1 Cor. 15:27,28.)

In addition, everything we do as individuals has consequences — some bad, some good, depending on the "seed" sown. Some of those consequences may mean individual tough times that affect others around us.

Do you realize that everything you do or say affects someone else? Periodically we all go through tough times, personally or as part of a community.

Those caught in the Christmas 2004 earthquake and tsunami are living in a truly tough time. Death, sickness and disease, poverty, famine, and destitution are the norm now in those countries.

Yes, they are receiving aid from all over the world. However, the ones who not only survive but prosper are those who *put the past behind them*, trust God, and move on.

Don't Live in the Past

In tough times, do not let yourself become so derailed thinking of the past that you sit on a siding while the rest of the train of life passes you by.

The "good old days" tend to be glamorized, many times exaggerated and enhanced by emotion out of proportion. The truth is that there are good and bad things about any "days."

Someone has said that you cannot have a better tomorrow if you focus on yesterday. You cannot reach the top of the mountain by looking backward down into the valley. Looking backward usually causes you to slide backwards.

Perhaps the most important thing to keep in mind in tough times is: *do not quit*. Don't give up. Trust God for a better tomorrow.

Don't Quit!

The Rev. Robert Schuller says, "Most people who succeed in the face of seemingly impossible conditions are people who simply do not know how to quit."[1]

The most successful men have been those who spell failure "o-p-p-o-r-t-u-n-i-t-y."

Whether good or bad, overflow or scarcity, each will pass and give way to the other. In a year of good harvests, it is time to increase the sowing, not pull back because there is hope for the future.

A year of overflow of bad resulting from sowing sparsely or not taking care of crops is an even better time to repent than in an overflow of good. Repent, if necessary, and sow as much as possible in order to be ready for the next good harvest time.

Think about a farmer who has lost his crop one year through natural disasters and perhaps

---

[1]Maxwell, *Leadership 101*; p. 41.

lost a child in the same tornado. Would you advise him to give up on life?

Suppose he said, "We lost our harvest. We lost a child. We lost our home. We're going to cut down this year on what we sow and live in tents. Everything happens to us. We can't expect anything good." Would that man recover from a tough time?

When hard times come, it is no help to operate according to the world's thinking.

When times are tough, it is the perfect time to "prove" God and His Word. (Mal. 3:10.) He is the only Rock in a "weary land." (Isa. 32:2, a prophetic word of Jesus.)

When times are tough is the very point at which children of God should "plant" more than ever before. Psalms 126:5 says: **They that sow in tears shall reap in joy.** Absolutely do not hold back on giving when you are experiencing tough times. Withholding seed only makes bad matters worse.

Above all, *don't give up hope*, particularly in tough times. It is easy to be hopeful when things are going well. However, in good times, you really do not need hope. *Hope* is the expectation that what you need, want, or desire will come to pass.

Without hope, you cannot have faith in God's promises.

Without hope, you succumb to the devil's biggest weapon: discouragement.

Without hope, you fall into self-pity and begin to think, "Well life is not fair. It is no use trying. How can I prosper when the economy is down the drain? It's the Democrats' — or the Republicans' — fault."

Ultimately, that state of mind for a Christian leads to blaming God for an imperfect world. You might call that attitude "cutting off your nose to spite your face," or spitting in the face of the only One who can help you.

Studying the Word of God will give you the knowledge that *in God*, we can always have hope. He will never leave us or forsake us. (Heb. 13:5.) Without His mercy and grace, this world would be forever in tough times, not just intermittently.

Also, I have to tell you an absolute truth: *Life is not fair for most people*. However, living according to God's principles evens the playing field, balances the odds, and gives us stepping

Don't Quit!

stones across the raging waters as well as through the calm streams.

The Apostle James wrote: **Consider it all joy, my brethren, when you encounter various trials, knowing that the testing of your faith produces endurance. And let endurance have its perfect result, that you may be perfect and complete, lacking in nothing** (James 1:2-4 *NAS.*)

Tough times are never a waste, unless you moan and groan through them and throw away the chance to develop patience and faith through hope and endurance. Life certainly is not a level playing field, but is made up of hills and valleys, rivers to cross, and mountains to climb.

If your eyes are on Jesus and not yourself, good times or tough times both are part of the foreign landscape through which we travel looking for a far country where we really belong. (Heb. 11:9,10.) Abraham had prosperous times and tough times. So did the other Bible patriarchs. *Tough times are not exclusive to you.*

Particularly in tough times, it pays to look up at Jesus, not around at other people.

15

Don't Focus on Others

If your eyes are on those around you, it is likely you will end up in the ditch!

Another absolutely true saying is that "God plus one is a majority." It does not matter who is against you if God is for you, the Apostle Paul wrote. (Rom. 8:31b.) However, it helps to find out where God is and get on *His* side rather than deciding your own path and begging Him to be on *your* side.

Following others, especially those not following Jesus, makes a mockery of many verses in Psalms that reflect the focus of King David in tough times, such as Psalm 34:6 *NAS*: **This poor man cried and the Lord heard him, and saved him out of all his troubles.**

Notice that David did not write that God would save that man *from* troubles, but *out of them*. You have to be in trouble before you can be saved out of it. Nor did any Bible writer say that following other people would save you or deliver you.

The Apostle Paul said to follow him, *but only as he followed Jesus* (1 Cor. 11:1), so he was simply showing people Jesus' ways and direction. He was not building a following for himself.

Other people can be mentors, role models, and even be saintly. However, they will be helpful to you only if you know that what you see in them worth following is *the way in which they are like Jesus*.

How can you know what Jesus was like? It is easy, because the Holy Spirit told us about Jesus through earthly writers. He is the Author of the Bible; men were the writers. Study the Gospels thoroughly and ask God to give you understanding of why and how Jesus acted.

You cannot understand Him or the Bible with the natural mind, because spiritual things appear as foolishness to one blinded to the Spirit. (1 Cor. 2:14-16.) It is necessary to first become born again, adopted into the family of God. (John 3:16; Rom. 10:9,10.)

After that, you still will not immediately be able to read with spiritual eyes, but you have a starting place which non-believers do not have.

Join what I call the "Five O'Clock Club,"* and before long, it will seem as if scriptures are being illuminated to you. Even now, after years of reading the Bible, I sometimes see something and say, "Wow, I didn't know that was in there!"

To focus on something means everything else is in your peripheral vision.

Following Jesus and not looking to other people, even great leaders, feels as if you are swimming upstream. However, "going with the flow" of the world in tough times means ending up being washed over the dam or mired in the mud somewhere.

Jesus lived in tough times. The nation of Judah was under foreign occupation, taxed by Rome and governed by Rome. The religious leaders opposed Him.

He had no permanent home although even the "foxes have dens," He said. (Matt. 8:20; Luke 9:58.) He endured persecution as Christians in America have not yet had to do. However, Jesus was confident the Father would provide for His needs. (Matt. 6:28.) In fact, He had finances on His journeys because there was enough money for Judas to carry a money bag. (John 12:6, 13:29.)

An old childhood tale is about an emperor who was conned into going out in public naked while declaring his clothes were the best to be seen. It took an innocent child to say, "The emperor has no clothes!" The adults, through fear of being different from others around them, kept insisting the emperor's clothes were the finest ever seen.

Getting your eyes off Jesus and on the crowd can cause you to stumble and make tough times tougher. It can cause you to think the emperor has clothes, when he has none.

Above all, in tough times, do not slip into negative thinking or negative emotions. By negative, I mean any thought that raises itself against the Word (2 Cor. 10:5) or gives rise to fear, doubt, fretting or worry.

Hundreds of my partners join me in getting up at 5 a.m. each day and reading two chapters in the Old Testament, five in Psalms, one in Proverbs, and two in the New Testament. This daily time of reading, prayer, and meditation in the Word makes all the difference to my day. I know it will have the same effect on your day. Try it and see!

Don't Worry, Fret, or Despair

Worry makes a veil between you and God. Ruth Bell Graham wrote that worry and worship of God cannot co-exist, because they are "mutually exclusive."[1] Someone else said that worry is paying interest on a loan that you may never borrow.

There is no point in bemoaning the times or a personal tragedy and crying, "Why me?" God did not fall off His throne because of what happened to you, nor will your anger at him or your despair knock Him off.

Look to Him to put you back on your feet. Grieve over a personal loss and then set yourself in Him to get through it and go on with life. Your life is not over. Don't waste what is left of your time on earth.

That does not mean I cannot sympathize with those going through personal tragedy and

---

[1] *The Quotable Christian,* Favorite Quotes From Notable Christians compiled by Helen Hosier. (Ulrichsville, Ohio: Barbour Publishing, 1948), p. 208.

tough times. I do, because I have been there. I know what hard times are like. However, the way to walk through them, I have found, is to focus on God's love, mercy, and promises. *There always is a rainbow after the rain.*

Okay, so things may not ever be as they were in the past. However, as long as there is a future and you rest in God, the future can be good. History repeats itself: good times, bad times, over and over.

It is excruciating to lose a loved one, but this life is not all there is. If that loved one is with God, rejoice in the homegoing even if it seems way too soon to you.

Do not let "Job's Comforters" around you say, "Well, God gives and God takes away," and encourage you to lose your faith and hope in God. Also, don't let others put you under a guilt trip of lack of faith, "you-must-have-sin-in-your-life," or you deserve what happened to you. That also comes from "Job's Comforters."

If you read the last chapters of Job, you will see that sort of advice got those counselors in trouble with God, when all the time, they thought they were racking up points in Heaven!

If you have not already studied biblical economics, to which the world's ways are backward, then it is imperative to learn now what God has said about getting out of tough times.

If those called by His name followed His advice in tough times, offerings to churches and ministries doing His work in the world would go up instead of down as they did after 9/11.

It is not to the credit of Christians that the percentage of those who were tithing dropped from 20 percent to 10 or 12 percent then. It is not to the credit of the Church that even before 9/11 only about 20 percent of those calling themselves Christians were tithing.

Tough times can help you get a clear picture of what is really important in life.

The Apostle James gave us the primary key to use in tough times: **Is any one of you in trouble? He should pray** (James 5:13a *NIV.*) Add that advice to Luke's admonition, **For with God nothing shall be impossible** (Luke 1:37), and you will have direction enough to get you out of any situation.

If you get into fear, you may sit down *on the track* and get run over for fear of moving in any direction.

If you panic, you get in too big a hurry to be wise, and you may do rash things that quite often make bad matters worse.

The late Mrs. Charles E. Cowman, who wrote well-known devotional books of the early 20th century, wrote:[2]

In times of uncertainty, wait.

Always, if you have any doubt, wait.

Do not force yourself to any action.

If you have a restraint in your spirit,
   wait until all is clear, and do not go
   against it.

If you will praise and worship God in tough times, it will make all the difference, not just to your attitude and state of mind but to your hope and faith.

It is imperative in tough times to speak positively. In other words, speak what God has said for tough circumstances. Remember: life and death are in the power of the tongue. (Prov.

---

[2]Ibid, p. 106.

18:21.) Other biblical facts about the power of the tongue are:

- **The tongue of the wise is health** (Prov. 12:18b).

- **The tongue of the wise useth knowledge aright: but the mouth of fools poureth out foolishness** (Prov. 15:2).

Would you rather have the results of being wise in tough times, or the results of having the foolishness of doubt and disbelief coming out of your mouth?

- **A wholesome tongue is a tree of life** (Prov. 15:4a).

- **Whoso keepeth his mouth and his tongue keepeth his soul from troubles** (Prov. 21:23).

"Confessing the answer" does not mean pretending there is no problem. Positive thinking based on falsehood is useless, even counter productive.

Jesus said faith could move mountains, but it won't work if you stand there saying, "There is no mountain. There is no mountain." *Speak to your mountain in faith and sooner or later, it will move.* (Mark 11:23,24.) God's Word never fails.

One thing many Christians overlook in their lives is unforgiveness. Somehow they think they have a right to condemn and hold offenses against someone they feel has harmed them.

However, the Bible says unforgiveness is as much a problem to God as any of the carnal things. (Matt. 6:14,15.)

They do not "feel" like forgiving someone who has "done them wrong." Let me tell you a fact you may not know:

Forgiveness is a choice of your will; forgiveness is not a feeling! Unforgiveness is a sin.

Forgive first, and the release from bitterness and resentment will follow. If you wait until you feel like forgiving someone, it will never happen.

Ten Dos and Don'ts for Tough Times

1. Do pray without ceasing, putting your trust in the Lord as you begin to speak forth His promises.
2. Do repent of any sins or shortcomings, taking responsibility for any part you had in causing the tough times.
3. Do forgive anyone who has injured you, and above all, forgive yourself because God forgave you when you repented. (Mark 11:25,26.) Forgive others so your prayers may be answered.
4. Do praise and worship God, for He is your Rescuer, your hope, and your comfort.
5. Do keep your eyes on Jesus and not others.
6. Don't pray the problem; pray the answer.
7. Don't pretend there is no problem or no tough times. If everything is fine, why are you in trouble?

8. Don't give in to negative emotions that cause doubt and disbelief, and above all, don't panic!

9. Don't — whatever you do — cut back on your giving. If at all possible, increase your tithes and offerings. In financial tough times, *giving is one of your biggest weapons to "blow a hole" in the wall of hardship in front of you.* Your tithes should go to the ministry or place where you receive spiritual food.

10. Don't forget the spiritual armor the Apostle Paul told us we have. (Eph. 6:14-16.) In tough times you need the whole armor of God to **be strong in the Lord, and in the power of his might** (Eph. 6:11). The armor consists of:

- The helmet of salvation.

- The righteousness of Jesus so we do not rely on our own righteousness. (Isa. 64:6.)

- The truth of God found in His Word.

- The preparation of the gospel of peace.

- The shield of faith.
- The sword of the Spirit, which is the Word of God.

Notice that *faith is your shield*, not a sword. Faith is to defend your position by standing in confidence that God has the answer. *The sword is the Word of God.* Stand your ground and use your weapon against the enemy, whose fiery darts include those negative thoughts of defeat.

In the world of body-building, "hard gaining" is a term used for all of the exercise that makes up the work necessary to achieve the end result of a fit and healthy body. Patient endurance in the world of athletics is called "no pain, no gain."

Spiritual maturity is not achieved without patience. Patience, however, must be based on the confidence that Jesus, not self, is your strength through exercises of tests and trials that constitute "spiritual body-building."

Well-known minister and author, Dr. J. I. Packer wrote:

> Patient endurance is most apparent when we stand steady under pain

and pressure instead of cutting and running, or crumpling and collapsing. But hanging tough in this way is a habit that takes some learning. The hardness of the gaining that produces Christian character must not be minimized: to endure Christianity . . . is no casual agenda.[1]

Endurance in tough times can bring great rewards in spiritual terms.

---

[1]Packer, Dr. J. I. *Rediscovering Holiness*, (Ann Arbor, MI: Vine Books, an imprint of Servant Publications; Copyright 1992 by J.I. Packer), p. 241.

About the Author

Born a coal miner's son in rural Arkansas, Tom Leding cannot remember when he did not have a burning desire to make good in the world in order to serve God. Against heavy odds, he earned college and doctorate degrees while becoming one of Tulsa's most noted businessmen.

As he learned to apply the prosperity principles in the Bible through hard work and diligence, he rose to the top of the field in every endeavor he tried. From chief accountant at American Airlines to becoming top salesman out of Farmer's Insurance Company's 14,000 national agents to running his own full-service insurance agency with a staff of 10 brokers, he never lost sight of Who was His Source and real Boss.

Now, he feels his mandate is to lead God's people out of poverty into prosperity. He is much sought after as a teacher in churches, conferences, and on television programs. Also, he is the author of eight books.

Tom and his wife Sue live in Tulsa, as does their son Ron, his wife Carol, and their two children, Adam and Rebecca.

The Tom Leding Ministries Vision

Proclaiming the truth and power
of the Gospel of Jesus Christ
with excellence;

challenging Christians to
live victoriously,
grow spiritually,
know God intimately,
and to receive all the blessings
God has in store for them.

Other Books and Tapes by Tom Leding

The Dynamic Laws of Creative Selling
Rags to Riches: You Don't Have To Be Poor
The Making of a King:
How To Rise Above Your Circumstances
Prosperity Is Your Inheritance
Your Greatest Asset
Who Said That?
How To Defeat Giants of Poverty
Tithing Is Not Optional
Wisdom for Success in Life (audio)
Selected Prosperity Scriptures CD

* * *

To Contact the Author, write
Tom Leding
4412 S. Harvard
Tulsa, OK 74135
Or call
1-800-880-8220
Or e-mail
TomLeding@yahoo.com
When you write, please include your testimony
of how this book has helped you.
Your Prayer requests are welcome.
www.TomLeding.com